Sovereign Debt in Advanced Economies: Overview and Issues for Congress

Rebecca M. Nelson
Analyst in International Trade and Finance

January 31, 2013

Congressional Research Service

7-5700

www.crs.gov

R41838

CRS Report for Congress
Prepared for Members and Committees of Congress

Summary

Sovereign debt, also called public debt or government debt, refers to debt incurred by governments. Since the global financial crisis of 2008-2009, public debt in advanced economies has increased substantially. A number of factors related to the financial crisis have fueled the increase, including fiscal stimulus packages, the nationalization of private-sector debt, and lower tax revenue. Even if economic growth reverses some of these trends, such as by boosting tax receipts and reducing spending on government programs, aging populations in advanced economies are expected to strain government debt levels in coming years.

High levels of debt in advanced economies are a relatively new global concern, after decades of attention on debt levels in developing and emerging markets. Three Eurozone countries, Greece, Ireland, and Portugal, have turned to the International Monetary Fund (IMF) and other European governments for financial assistance in order to avoid defaulting on their loans. There are also concerns about the sustainability of public debt in Japan and the United States.

To date, many advanced-economy governments have embarked on fiscal austerity programs (such as cutting spending and/or increasing taxes) to address historically high levels of debt. This policy response has been criticized by some economists as possibly undermining a weak recovery from the global financial crisis. Others argue that the austerity plans do not go far enough, and that more reforms are necessary to bring debt levels down, especially considering the aging populations in many countries.

Issues for Congress

- **Is the United States headed for a Eurozone-style debt crisis?** Some economists and Members of Congress fear that, given historically high levels of U.S. public debt, the United States is headed towards a debt crisis similar to those experienced by some Eurozone countries. Others argue that important differences between the United States and Eurozone economies, such as growth rates, borrowing rates, and type of exchange rate (floating or fixed), put the United States in a stronger position. The United States has a long historical record of debt repayment, and bond spreads indicate that investors currently view the United States as far less risky than Greece, Ireland, or Portugal.

- **Impact on U.S. economy.** The focus of most advanced economies on austerity programs to lower debt levels could slow growth in advanced economies and depress demand for U.S. exports. Financial instability stemming from high debt levels could also impact U.S. markets and financial institutions.

- **Policy options for Congress.** Congress is debating proposals to reduce federal debt levels in the United States. Congress could urge the Administration to coordinate fiscal policies multilaterally to avoid simultaneous austerity measures that undermine the economic recovery.

Contents

Figures

Tables

Appendixes

Contacts

Introduction

In many advanced economies, the global financial crisis of 2008-2009 and ensuing recession resulted in large fiscal stimulus packages, the nationalization of private-sector debt, lower tax revenue, and higher government spending.[1] These factors led to large budget deficits and increased borrowing by governments from capital markets in order to fund these deficits. **Figure 1** shows the rapid increase in public debt as a percentage of GDP in the major G-7 economies (Canada, France, Germany, Italy, Japan, the United Kingdom, and the United States) following the financial crisis. For the G-7 economies, sovereign debt rose from 84% of GDP in 2006 to a forecasted 125% of GDP in 2012.

Figure 1. G-7 Public Debt as a Percentage of GDP, 1991 - present

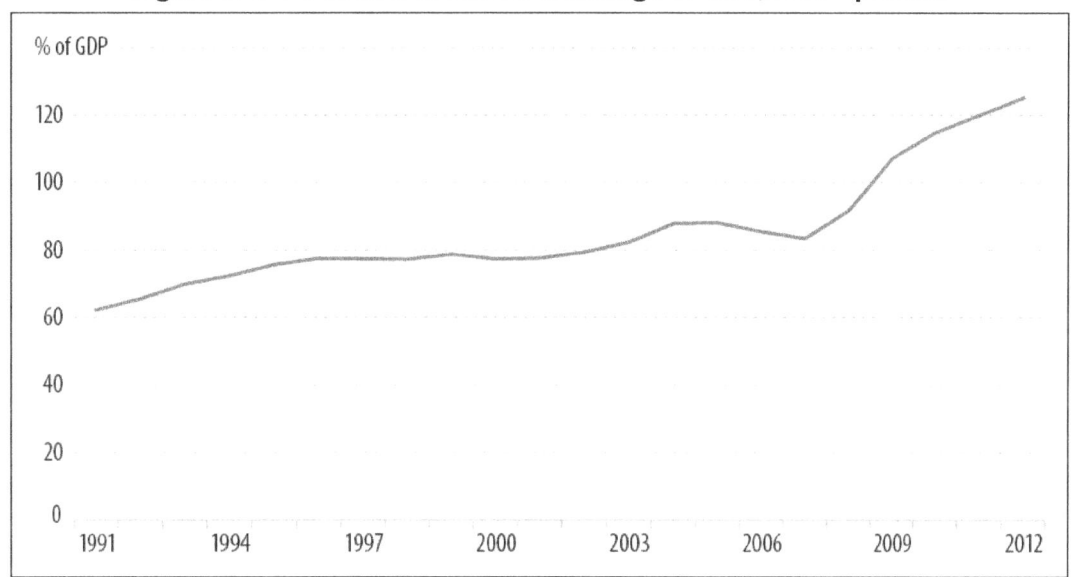

Source: *IMF World Economic Outlook*, October 2012.

Concerns about high levels of public debt have been most focused on the Eurozone, where a debt crisis has been ongoing since late 2009.[2] Three Eurozone countries—Greece, Ireland, and Portugal—have had to borrow money from other European countries and the International

---

[1] This report uses the IMF's definition of advanced economies: Australia, Austria, Belgium, Canada, Cyprus, the Czech Republic, Denmark, Estonia, Finland, France, Germany, Greece, Hong Kong, Iceland, Ireland, Israel, Italy, Japan, Korea, Luxembourg, Malta, Netherlands, New Zealand, Norway, Portugal, Singapore, Slovak Republic, Slovenia, Spain, Sweden, Switzerland, Taiwan, the United Kingdom, and the United States. According to the IMF, their classification "is not based on strict criteria, economic or otherwise, and it has evolved over time." The IMF uses three major criteria to classify economies as advanced: (1) per capita income level; (2) export diversification; and (3) degree of integration into the global financial system. For more information, see the Statistical Appendix of the IMF World Economic Outlook (http://www.imf.org/external/pubs/ft/weo/2011/01/pdf/statapp.pdf) and the IMF World Economic Outlook Data Forum (http://forums.imf.org/showthread.php?t=154).

[2] The Eurozone refers to the group of 17 European Union (EU) countries that uses the euro (€) as its national currency. For more on the Eurozone crisis, see CRS Report R42377, *The Eurozone Crisis: Overview and Issues for Congress*, coordinated by Rebecca M. Nelson.

Monetary Fund (IMF) in order to meet obligations and avoid defaulting on their debt. There are also concerns about the sustainability of their public finances in Spain and Italy, much larger economies in the Eurozone. However, concerns over rising debt levels are not limited to Eurozone countries. Debates about the public debt are central features of political discourse in the United States, Japan, and the United Kingdom, among others.

High levels of sovereign debt in advanced economies are of interest to Congress for a number of reasons. First, the IMF has identified advanced economy debt as a possible threat to the global economic recovery,[3] as countries struggle to find a balance between growth and debt management in an uncertain global economic recovery. Second, Congress has and continues to debate a number of budget and debt issues, particularly in the context of the agreement reached on the debt ceiling and federal budget. In many of these fiscal debates, parallels are drawn between the United States and other advanced economies, such as Greece, Ireland, and the United Kingdom. Analyzing debt levels and factors that shape debt sustainability can help inform these comparisons. Third, how other countries reduce their debt impacts the U.S. economy. Most advanced economies are implementing fiscal austerity programs to lower their debt levels. Simultaneous austerity programs in the advanced countries, the United States' major trading partners, could depress demand for U.S. exports abroad, as well as deter investment in and from advanced economies.

This report proceeds as follows:

- The first section provides background information on sovereign debt, including why governments borrow, how sovereign debt differs from private debt, why governments repay their debt (or not), and how sovereign debt is measured.

- The second section examines the shift of concerns over sovereign debt sustainability from emerging markets in the 1990s and 2000s to advanced economies following the global financial crisis of 2008-2009, and the challenges posed by high debt levels.

- The third section analyzes the different policy options governments have for lowering debt levels. It also discusses the current strategy being used by most advanced economies—fiscal austerity—and concerns that have been raised about its global impact.

- Finally, the fourth section analyzes issues of particular interest to Congress, including comparisons between U.S. and European debt levels, how efforts to reduce debt levels could impact the U.S. economy, and policy options available to Congress for engaging on this issue.

---

[3] Dominique Strauss-Kahn (then-Managing Director of the IMF), "Financial Crisis and Sovereign Risk: Implications for Financial Stability," remarks for IMF High-Level Roundtable, March 18, 2011, http://www.imf.org/external/np/speeches/2011/031811.htm.

Background Definitions and Concepts

Why and How Governments Borrow

Sovereign debt, also called public debt or government debt, refers to debt incurred by governments.[4] Governments borrow money for a number of different reasons, such as health, education, defense, infrastructure, and research. Some borrowing is for consumption, while other borrowing is for investment. Governments may also borrow in order to run expansionary fiscal policies (such as increasing spending or cutting taxes), with the goal of increasing economic activity, spurring economic growth, and decreasing unemployment.

Most economists believe that public debt can play a productive role in the economy under certain circumstances. They argue, for example, that borrowing by the government can help stimulate the economy during a recession or fund long-term investment projects that increase economic output in the future. However, they also caution that governments do not always use debt prudently. Many economists argue that governments may be reluctant to increase taxes or cut spending during economic booms in order to pay off debt incurred during economic downturns, leading to growing debt levels over time. They also caution that governments may borrow for consumption purposes, and that this type of borrowing can create difficulties when the debt obligation falls due, because it does not yield future economic benefits.

Today, the governments of most advanced economies, as well as some emerging markets, borrow money by issuing government bonds and selling them to private investors. They may sell bonds to private investors overseas or to domestic investors. Some countries, such as Japan and Italy, sell a sizeable portion of their bonds to investors at home. The United States does both, with approximately half of its federal debt held by foreigners.[5] Some emerging and developing economies also borrow from other governments and international organizations, such as the World Bank and the IMF.

How Sovereign Debt Differs from Private Debt

Sovereign debt differs from private-sector debt, or debt incurred by households and corporations, for two reasons. First, there is no international bankruptcy court that can enforce debt contracts between private investors and sovereign governments. In the domestic context, private borrowers cannot simply refuse to repay debts to creditors. Domestic laws and courts can force debtors to turn over existing assets to creditors or put the debtor through bankruptcy proceedings, during which the borrower liquidates its assets and turns them over to the creditor. In the international context, by contrast, there are no internationally accepted laws or bankruptcy courts to provide

---

[4] Government debt, public debt, and sovereign debt are used interchangeably in this report. Sovereign debt is related to, but different from, government deficits. A government deficit occurs when government spending exceeds government revenue in a particular year. If spending is less than revenue, the government runs a surplus for that year. If the government runs a deficit, it borrows to finance the deficit spending, and the deficit adds to the government's overall debt level. The deficit is a "flow" of borrowing that increases the "stock" of debt.

[5] For data on foreign holdings of U.S. public debt, see U.S. Department of the Treasury, "Major Foreign Holdings of Treasury Securities," http://www.treasury.gov/resource-center/data-chart-center/tic/Documents/mfh.txt. For total U.S. public debt, see U.S. Department of the Treasury, "Monthly Statement of the Public Debt of the United States," http://www.treasurydirect.gov/govt/reports/pd/mspd/mspd.htm.

creditors recourse against governments that refuse to repay their debts. Debt contracts between governments and private creditors often include provisions that stipulate what jurisdiction's law is to be applied in the event of a dispute about the contract. However, there is no way to force a government that has defaulted on its debt to abide by another country's court ruling that it must repay the loan.[6] Proposals for creating internationally accepted bankruptcy proceedings and regulations, possibly to be overseen by the IMF, have not been fruitful.[7]

A second reason why public debt differs from some private debt contracts is that sovereign debt is "unsecured," or not backed by collateral. Governments cannot credibly commit to turn over assets if they are unable to repay their debts, because, again, there is no international authority to compel them do to so. This contrasts with the private sector, where debt contracts are frequently backed by collateral. For example, property serves as collateral for mortgages in most countries. Some private-sector debt is not backed by collateral. Credit card debt, for example, is unsecured.

This is not to say that public debt is inherently more risky than private debt. In fact, some credit rating agencies use the credit rating of the sovereign as an upper limit for the ratings that domestic borrowers in that country can receive. However, the strict use of a sovereign credit rating ceiling for domestic borrowers has waned in recent years.[8] Sovereign debt may be less risky than private-sector debt because governments have the power of taxation to raise money in order to service debt, unlike private borrowers.

Why Governments Repay Debt, and Why They Default

If creditors have limited recourse against governments that default, why do they lend to governments in the first place? It is generally argued that governments, even in the absence of international bankruptcy court and secured debt contracts, will want to repay their debts in order to build a good reputation in capital markets. Having a reputation for creditworthiness means that the government can continue to borrow from investors at low interest rates, because investors view the loan as having a low level of risk. If the government does not have a good reputation with creditors, creditors will require high interest rates to compensate for the risk entailed in the investment, or they will refuse to lend the government money at all.[9] Some empirical evidence

---

[6] However, parties can voluntarily submit to recourse, such as through the International Centre for Settlement of Investment Disputes (ICSID), a branch of the World Bank Group. Investors can also use the threat of legal "attachments" to prevent defaulted governments from re-entering capital markets until defaulted debt has been resolved. Attachments refer to a legal process by which a court designates specific property owned by the debtor in default to be transferred to the creditor. For more information, see Marcus Miller and Dania Thomas, "Sovereign Debt Restructuring: The Judge, the Vultures and Creditor Rights," *The World Economy*, vol. 30, no. 10 (2007), pp. 1491-1509; and CRS Report R41029, *Argentina's Defaulted Sovereign Debt: Dealing with the "Holdouts"*, by J. F. Hornbeck.

[7] Perhaps the most prominent proposal was in 2002, when then-IMF Deputy Managing Director Anne O. Krueger proposed creating a "sovereign debt restructuring mechanism" to make the process of sovereign default and restructuring of sovereign debts more predictable, smoother, and quicker. Anne O. Krueger, *A New Approach to Sovereign Debt Restructuring*, International Monetary Fund, April 2002, http://www.imf.org/external/pubs/ft/exrp/sdrm/eng/sdrm.pdf.

[8] See, e.g., Eduardo Borensztein and Patricio Valenzuela, "The Credit Rating Agencies and the Sovereign Ceiling," *Roubini*, October 4, 2007, http://www.roubini.com/latam-monitor/337/the_credit_rating_agencies_and_the_sovereign_ceiling.

[9] It has also been argued that creditors are willing to lend to foreign governments because they believe their own government will use military force to ensure repayment. However, the use of "gunboat diplomacy" to enforce debt contracts is generally believed to have fallen out of practice in the early 20th century. See Martha Finnemore, *The* (continued...)

---

also suggests that default can have adverse effects on international trade and economic growth, providing other incentives for governments to repay their debts.[10]

Despite these incentives to repay debt, there is a long history of governments suspending debt payments or falling behind on their debt payments, referred to as "defaulting" on their debt.[11] A "debt crisis" typically refers to a situation where a country is either unable or unwilling to pay its debt. A debt crisis may not result in an actual default if, for example, the IMF lends the government the money it needs to stay current in its debt obligations. However, many governments that do default find an orderly way to restructure their debt that is acceptable to markets. Debt restructuring refers to some reorganization of the debt, such as a reduction in principal or lowering of interest rate, that makes debt payment easier for the borrower but still entails some payments to creditors. A creditor may get less in a debt restructuring than was originally agreed, but this may be preferable to getting nothing.

Defaults and debt crises can be triggered by a number of different economic and political factors, including, but not limited to, economic recessions, fluctuations in the price of imports and exports, currency depreciation (if debt is not payable in domestic currency), wars, and changes in political leadership. Debates over why governments default are typically framed in terms of a government's "ability" to repay versus a government's "willingness" to repay. For example, a government may be unable to repay debt denominated in foreign currency if it does not have sufficient access to foreign exchange. By contrast, a government may be unwilling to repay debt incurred under a previous regime, even if it has the resources to do so.

Measuring Sovereign Debt

A nation's debt burden is usually reported as a percentage of the country's gross domestic product (GDP), which indicates the size of the country's economy. Scaling debt to the size of the economy provides some indication of the government's relative debt burden, since it is expected that countries with bigger economies can sustain higher levels of debt in absolute terms than smaller economies.

Data on sovereign debt are reported in a number of different ways. They can be reported for the central government only, or for all levels of government (central/federal, state/province, and local governments, often called "general government debt"). For countries with high levels of spending by regional governments, such as Spain, there can be large differences between central government debt and general government debt. By convention, the headline number cited in news reports as the "U.S. debt" typically refers to the federal government debt only. Because of

---

(...continued)

Purpose of Intervention: Changing Beliefs about the Use of Force (Ithaca, NY: Cornell University Press, 2003). Also, some argue that creditors are willing to lend to governments because they can seize the government's assets overseas if the government fails to repay. In practice, however, it is argued that governments have few assets in foreign jurisdictions that can be seized by creditors, raising questions about the usefulness of that explanation. See Ugo Panizza, Federico Sturzenegger, and Jeromin Zettelmeyer, "The Economics and Law of Sovereign Debt and Default," *Journal of Economic Literature*, vol. 47, no. 3 (2009), pp. 1-47.

[10] E.g., see Andrew K. Rose, "One Reason Countries Pay Their Debts: Renegotiation and International Trade," *Journal of Development Economics*, vol. 77, no. 1 (2005), pp. 189-206; Eduardo Borensztein and Ugo Panizza, *The Costs of Sovereign Default*, IMF Working Paper, WP/08/238, http://www.imf.org/external/pubs/ft/wp/2008/wp08238.pdf.

[11] See Carmen Reinhart and Kenneth Rogoff, *This Time Is Different: Eight Centuries of Financial Folly* (Princeton, NJ: Princeton University Press, 2009).

---

different accounting practices in the European Union (EU), general government debt is typically reported in news reports about EU debt levels. Some international organizations, such as the IMF and the Organization for Economic Cooperation and Development (OECD), report debt data for advanced economies that are standardized across countries.

Public debt can also be reported on a gross basis, referring to the government's total liabilities, or on a net basis, referring to the government's total financial liabilities minus the government's financial assets.[12] For governments with large financial assets, this can make a big difference. Japan's gross general government debt in 2012 is estimated to be 237% of GDP, but its net general government debt was almost half that (135% of GDP).[13] In contrast, forecasted Greece gross general government debt equaled its forecasted net general government debt in 2012; both were 171% of GDP.[14]

Finally, there is often interest in who holds the government's debt: foreign or domestic investors. As discussed above, some advanced economies sell most of their bonds to their citizens while others sell to foreigners. Italy and Japan, for example, sell large portions of their bonds to domestic investors. To address this issue, "external" public debt, or government debt owed to foreign creditors, is sometimes distinguished from "domestic" public debt, or government debt owed to domestic creditors.

Sovereign Debt Statistics: Key Terms

Level of Government

- *General government debt:* Debt for all levels of government (central/federal, state/province, and local governments)

- *Central government debt:* Debt of the central government

Inclusion of Government Assets

- *Gross government debt:* The government's total financial liabilities

- *Net government debt:* The government's total financial liabilities minus the government's total financial assets

Type of Creditor

- *External public debt:* Government debt owed to foreign creditors

- *Domestic public debt:* Government debt owed to domestic creditors

---

Many analysts warn that data on government debt should be used cautiously. They argue that governments do not account properly for all their financial obligations, and that if these hidden debts were included, estimates of government debts could be substantially higher.[15] Data on public debt levels are generally self-reported, and although there are international standards for data reporting, governments have some discretion about what is included on their balance sheet. For example, analysts caution that governments may not include their loan guarantees,

---

[12] Financial assets of the government refer to non-physical assets, such as securities, certificates, or bank deposits that belong to the government. Financial assets do not include all assets capable of being sold or activities capable of being taxed.

[13] *IMF World Economic Outlook,* October 2012.

[14] Ibid.

[15] See, e.g., Carmen Reinhart and Kenneth Rogoff, *From Financial Crash to Debt Crisis,* NBER Working Paper, No. 15795, March 2010, http://www.nber.org/papers/w15795.pdf; William Buiter, "The Debt of Nations," *Citi Investment Research & Analysis,* January 7, 2011.

obligations of state-owned enterprises, obligations of the central bank, or implicit guarantees in their data reports. Some governments may also underreport data. In the Greek debt crisis, for example, revelations of underreported budget deficits contributed to investor anxiety surrounding the sustainability of Greece's debt. Some economists also argue that some governments do not fully account for spending on government programs for aging citizens, such as pensions and health care, in their budget projections, leading to substantial underestimates of future debt levels.[16]

Trends in Sovereign Debt

Pre-Crisis: Vulnerabilities in Emerging Markets

In the decades leading up to the global financial crisis of 2008-2009, concerns over sovereign debt had been concentrated on middle-income, emerging-market countries. For example, the 1980s Latin American debt crisis, Russia's financial crisis in 1998, and Argentina's default in 2001 were major debt crises that received high levels of international attention and financial support. Several emerging markets also restructured their debt in the late 1990s and 2000s, including Russia, Ukraine, Pakistan, Ecuador, Argentina, Moldova, and Uruguay, among others.[17]

Emerging markets tended to be more susceptible to debt crises than advanced economies for a number of reasons. High debt levels in some emerging markets, access to fewer resources to repay debt, volatility in commodity prices, and weak political institutions are often cited as factors. However, the structure of emerging-market debt contracts also made them more vulnerable. Emerging-market debt tends to be denominated in foreign currencies, such as U.S. dollars and euros, and tends to have shorter maturities.[18] This made emerging markets vulnerable to changes in the exchange rate, since a depreciation of the local currency could substantially increase the amount of the debt in terms of local currency. Short debt maturities also impacted their ability to "roll over" debt, or renew the loan upon maturity. Since the debt contracts were short term, the debt had to be rolled over more frequently, which could be difficult if investors lost confidence in the government. Advanced economies, by contrast, are able to borrow in domestic currency (for example, the U.S. government borrows in U.S. dollars) and their debt tends to have longer maturities. Because advanced economies do not bear exchange-rate risk and can roll over their debt less frequently, sovereign debt in advanced economies had generally been more stable than in emerging markets.

---

[16] See, e.g., Stephen G. Cecchetti, M. S. Mohanty, and Fabrizio Zampolli, *The Future of Public Debt: Prospects and Implications*, Bank for International Settlements (BIS), Working Paper No. 300, pp. 8-9, http://www.bis.org/publ/work300.pdf.

[17] Federico Sturzenegger and Jeromin Zettelmeyer, *Debt Defaults and Lessons from a Decade of Crises* (Cambridge, MA: MIT Press, 2007).

[18] Barry Eichengreen, Ricardo Hausmann, and Ugo Panizza, *Currency Mismatches, Debt Intolerance and Original Sin: Why They Are Not the Same and Why It Matters*, NBER Working Paper, No. 10036, October 2003, http://www.nber.org/papers/w10036.

Post-Crisis: Rising Debt Levels in Advanced Economies

Since the financial crisis, concerns over sovereign debt sustainability have shifted from emerging markets to advanced industrialized economies. In many advanced economies, the financial crisis accelerated rising levels of sovereign debt (see **Figure 1**). Governments extended financial support to troubled banks to stabilize the financial system, and enacted large stimulus packages to boost demand, output, and employment. The ensuing recession resulted in lower tax receipts and more government spending on programs such as unemployment insurance. All these factors combined to create a substantial increase in government debt among advanced industrialized countries. Some argue that if growth returned to the economy, debt levels would fall due to rising tax receipts and lower spending on programs such as unemployment insurance. Long-term trends, however, suggest that aging populations could strain public finances in advanced economies in coming years, and that public debt levels could continue to be a problem.

Figure 2. Public Debt Levels in Advanced Economies, Compared to Emerging and Developing Economies, 2000-2017

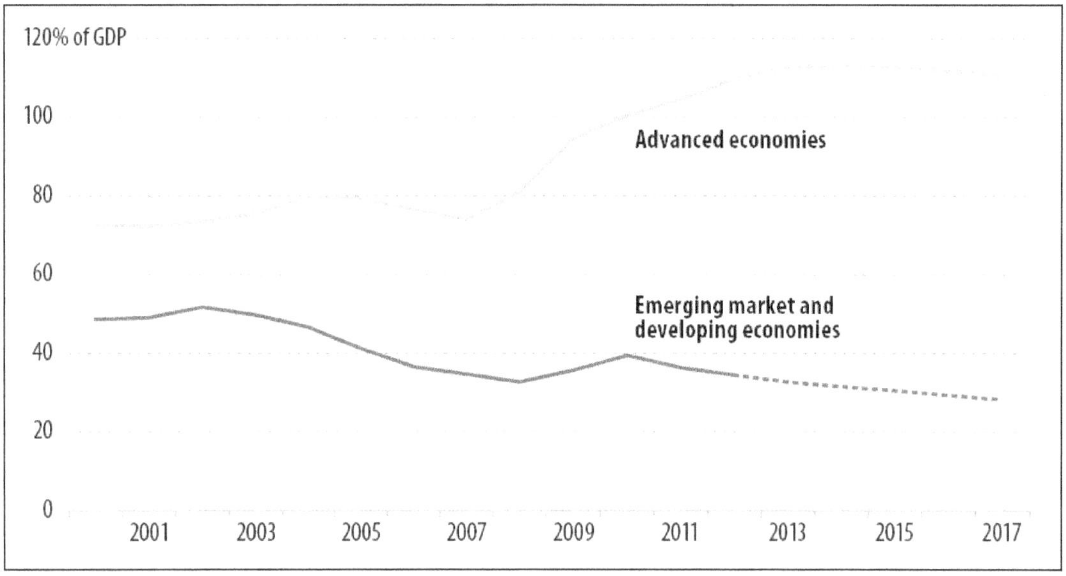

Source: *IMF World Economic Outlook*, October 2012.

Note: Gross general government debt. See **Table A-1** for more detailed data.

Specifically, **Figure 2** shows that gross general government debt in advanced economies increased slightly in the years before the global financial crisis, from 72% of GDP in 2000 to 77% of GDP in 2006. During the financial crisis, however, sovereign debt levels rose more rapidly, to 105% of GDP in 2011. The IMF forecasts that they will continue to increase through 2014, to 113% of GDP, before falling subsequently.

In contrast, debt levels in emerging markets and developing countries were lower than those in advanced economies in 2000. Emerging-market and developing-country gross general government debt was only 49%, compared to 72% of GDP in advanced economies. Moreover, emerging-market and developing-country debt has fallen fairly steadily over the past decade, from 52% of GDP in 2002 to 36% of GDP in 2011. By 2017, the IMF predicts that debt in emerging and developing countries will fall even further to 28% of GDP.

Variation Among Advanced Economies

Although public debt has generally been rising in advanced economies, there is wide variation among debt levels in advanced economies. **Figure 3** shows forecasted gross general government debt across advanced economies as a percentage of GDP in 2012. In that year, Japan is estimated to have the highest ratio of gross general government debt relative to GDP, at 237% of GDP. The second highest was Greece, at 171% of GDP. Estonia had the lowest level, at only 9% of GDP. The United States ranked sixth among advanced economies, just after Ireland and before Singapore, with an estimated gross general government debt of 107% of GDP. It is also worth noting that the three Eurozone countries experiencing the most severe market pressure—Greece, Ireland, and Portugal—have among the highest debt-to-GDP ratios among advanced economies, but other advanced economies, such as Japan, are facing much less market pressure. This fact highlights that markets consider a variety of indicators, not just debt levels, when evaluating a government's debt sustainability.

Figure 3. Gross General Government Debt in Advanced Economies, 2012

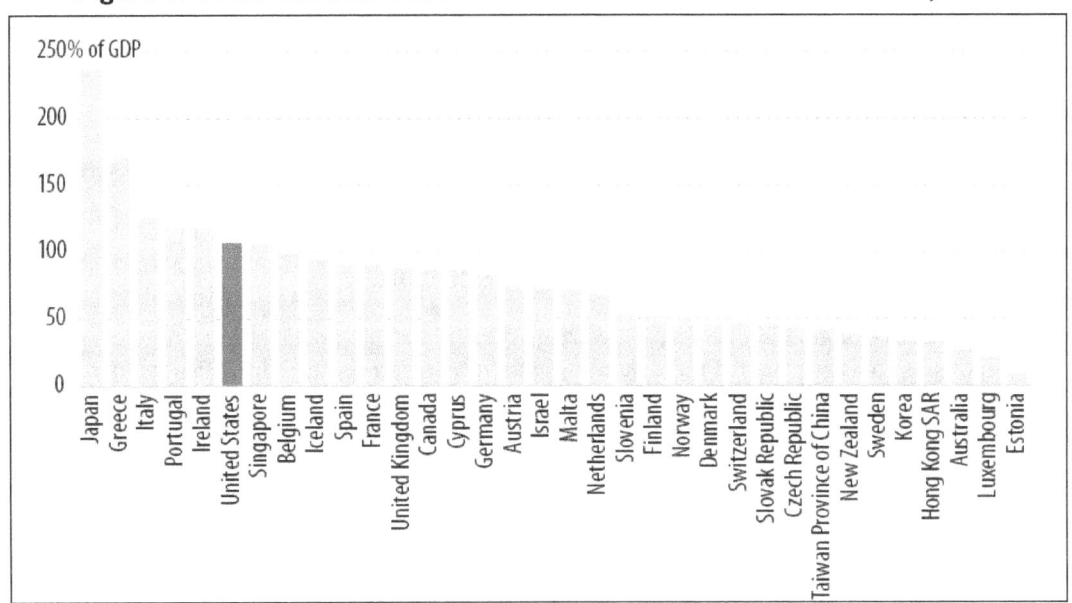

Source: *IMF World Economic Outlook*, October 2012.

Note: Forecasts. See **Table A-1** for more data on gross general government debt in advanced economies.

Net general government debt presents a slightly different ranking of debt levels among countries, as shown in **Figure 4**. By this measure, Greece is forecasted to be the most indebted economy in 2012, with a net general government debt of 171% of GDP, followed by Japan with 135% of GDP. Some countries, such as Norway and Finland, have negative net general government debt levels, because their financial assets are larger than their financial liabilities. U.S. net general government debt is estimated to be 84% of GDP in 2012. Of the countries where data on net debt are available, it ranked sixth among advanced economies, with net general government debt higher than France's but lower than Ireland's.

Figure 4. Net General Government Debt in Advanced Economies, 2012

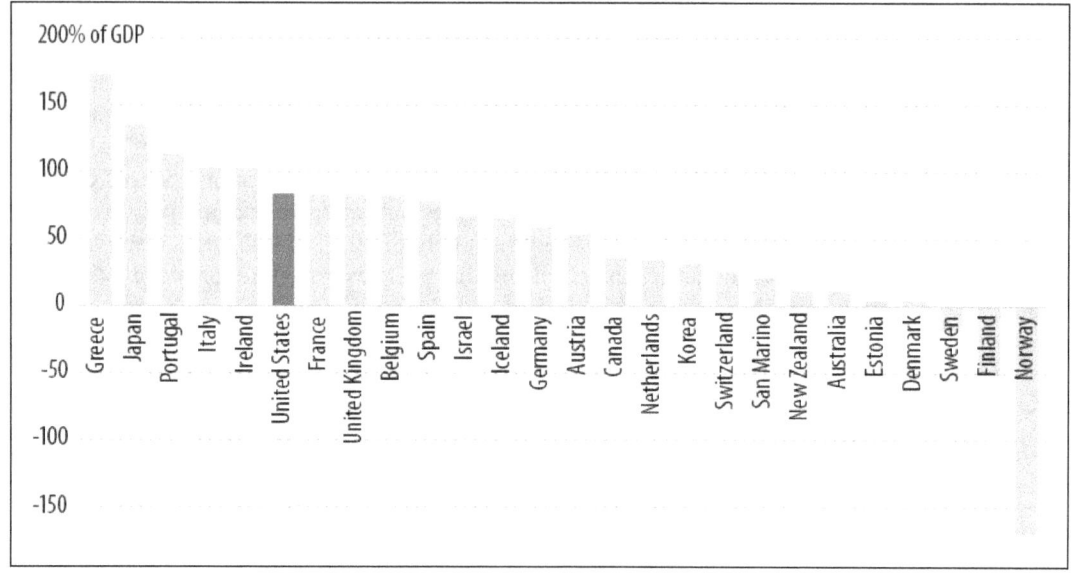

Source: *IMF World Economic Outlook*, October 2012.

Note: Forecasts. A negative net general government debt indicates that the government's total financial assets exceed the government's total financial liabilities. See **Table A-2** for more data on net general government debt in advanced economies.

Longer-Term Pressures in Advanced Economies

Some economists caution that the rise in sovereign debt among advanced economies during the financial crisis is only the start of more serious debt problems to come.[19] Specifically, there is concern that aging populations in many advanced economies will cause public debt to skyrocket, as a shrinking workforce will result in lower tax revenue while more retirees will require an increase in government spending on pensions and healthcare. Among OECD countries, for example, there were about 27 retirees for every 100 workers in 2000.[20] By 2050, the OECD forecasts about 62 retirees for every 100 workers.[21]

Economists at the Bank for International Settlements (BIS) suggest that the unfunded contingent liabilities associated with aging populations in advanced economies have not been definitively or comprehensively accounted for in government balance sheets or in budget and debt projections.[22] These economists argue that properly accounting for increases in age-related spending would result in significantly higher forecasts of debt levels. According to their calculations, debt-to-GDP

---

[19] See, e.g., Brian Keeley, "Debt—You Ain't Seen Nothing Yet," *OECD Insights*, April 1, 2010, http://oecdinsights.org/2010/04/01/debt-%E2%80%93-you-ain%E2%80%99t-seen-nothing-yet/.

[20] "Ratio of the Inactive Elderly Population Aged 65 and Over to the Labour Force," *OECD Factbook*, http://puck.sourceoecd.org/vl=1955252/cl=13/nw=1/rpsv/factbook2009/01/02/01/01-02-01-g1.htm. Retirees are defined as inactive elderly population over 65 years old.

[21] Ibid.

[22] Stephen G. Cecchetti, M. S. Mohanty, and Fabrizio Zampolli, *The Future of Public Debt: Prospects and Implications*, Bank for International Settlements (BIS), Working Paper No. 300, pp. 8-9, http://www.bis.org/publ/work300.pdf.

ratios could rise by 2020 to 300% of GDP in Japan, 200% of GDP in the United Kingdom, and 150% of GDP in Belgium, France, Ireland, Greece, Italy, and the United States. These forecasts are based on a number of assumptions about government policies, interest rates, and growth, and changes in these assumptions could result in very different (higher or lower) estimates.

Challenges Posed by High Levels of Debt

Historically high public debt levels in advanced economies, combined with the threat of additional debt increases due to age-related spending, have become a source of serious concern for a number of reasons. First, they make governments vulnerable to unexpected and quick changes in investor behavior. If investors begin to fear that the government may default on its existing debt obligations, they may start demanding higher interest rates or refuse to lend to the government at all.[23] Loss of market access or interest rates that are no longer affordable could cause the government to make quicker and more drastic policy adjustments, including tax increases and/or spending cuts, than would have been necessary otherwise. To date, three Eurozone countries (Greece, Ireland, and Portugal) have come under this type of market pressure. However, all three of these countries borrowed money from other European countries and the IMF in order to continue to make debt repayments, while providing time for the governments to implement reforms that improve each country's fiscal position and regain investor confidence.

Second, government competition for loans can increase interest rates when the economy is at full employment, causing private investment to fall. Because private investment is important for long-term economic growth, government budget deficits tend to reduce the economic growth rate. This phenomenon is often referred to as public debt "crowding out" private investment. However, to the extent that government deficits finance public investment, there may not be any necessary detriment to the rate of economic growth. Borrowing from foreign investors can help maintain domestic investment and mitigate the problems associated with crowding out, although this creates obligations for profits to flow overseas in the future.[24]

Third, high debt levels restrict the ability of the government to respond to unexpected crises, such as natural disasters. As debt levels rise and investors become more concerned about the sustainability of the debt in the country, the government may find that it cannot access the financing it needs to address a crisis, and that it has to rely on other policy tools or on international support. For example, governments with high debt may be more constrained in their ability to employ policy tools to blunt the impact of economic downturns. Japan may be facing such a situation, as its borrowing needs have increased for financing reconstruction following the earthquake, tsunami, and ensuing nuclear crisis in March 2011.[25] At least one credit rating agency, S&P, has expressed concern about Japan's plan to increase deficit spending.

---

[23] If investors think that the government will use inflation to reduce the value of the debt in terms of goods and services, they may demand: higher interest rates, inflation-indexed bonds (bonds where the principal is indexed to inflation), or denomination of the bond in a different currency.

[24] CBO, *Federal Debt and the Risk of a Fiscal Crisis*, July 27, 2010, http://www.cbo.gov/ftpdocs/116xx/doc11659/07-27_Debt_FiscalCrisis_Brief.pdf.

[25] For more on Japan's earthquake and tsunami, see CRS Report R41702, *Japan's 2011 Earthquake and Tsunami: Economic Effects and Implications for the United States*, coordinated by Dick K. Nanto.

Addressing High Debt Levels

Given the problems that persistent high levels of public debt can create, there has been focus on how governments can lower debt levels. Governments have five major policy tools at their disposal for addressing high debt levels: fiscal consolidation, debt restructuring, inflation, growth, and financial repression.[26] The pros and cons of each strategy are analyzed below, as well as the current strategies being pursued by the governments of advanced economies to address their debt levels.

Addressing High Debt Levels: Policy Options

- **Fiscal consolidation:** Using tax increases and/or government spending cuts to reduce government deficits and lower government borrowing. In this report, "fiscal consolidation" is used interchangeably with "fiscal austerity."

- **Debt restructuring:** Renegotiating the debt contract to lower payments for the borrower. This can take a number of forms, such as lowering the interest rate, extending the repayment period (maturity of the loan), and lowering the outstanding balance (principal) of the loan.

- **Inflation:** Using inflation to reduce the "real" value of the debt, meaning the value of the loan in terms of goods and services. If there is inflation, the nominal or face value of the loan purchases fewer goods and services than at the time the debt contract was agreed upon.

- **Growth:** Pursing reforms, such as increasing the flexibility of labor markets, in order to spur growth. Increasing growth lowers debt relative to GDP.

- **Financial repression:** Government policies that induce or force domestic investors to buy government bonds at artificially low interest rates. All else being equal, when real interest rates (the interest rate adjusted for inflation) are negative, debt-to-GDP falls.

Policy Options

Fiscal Consolidation

A government may lower high levels of sovereign debt through austerity or fiscal consolidation, which generally refers to policies that reduce the government budget deficit. These include tax increases, spending cuts, or some combination of the two.

Some argue that austerity programs are effective at reducing the debt by directly targeting the cause of high debt levels: government spending that is too high or tax revenue that is too low. Proponents of fiscal consolidation also argue that it can increase economic growth. They argue, for example, that credible commitments to austerity measures can increase investor confidence in the government and lower the interest rate charged by investors on government bonds. If lower borrowing costs for the government also reduce interest rates for consumers and firms, consumer

---

[26] For example, see, "Locking Up Your Money," *The Economist*, May 4, 2011. Also note that some analysts have suggested that Greece should respond to its debt crisis by defaulting on its debt and depreciating its currency, similar to Argentina in the early 2000s. They argue that it would stimulate exports and spur economic growth. However, Greece's debt is denominated in euros, and leaving the Eurozone in favor of a depreciated national currency would significantly *raise* the value of its debt in terms of national currency. Since it is not a strategy for *reducing* debt levels, this policy option is not discussed in this report. However, for more on the consequences of Greece exiting the Eurozone, see CRS Report R41411, *The Future of the Eurozone and U.S. Interests*, coordinated by Raymond J. Ahearn; and CRS Report R41167, *Greece's Debt Crisis: Overview, Policy Responses, and Implications*, coordinated by Rebecca M. Nelson.

spending and investment may increase, expanding economic output.[27] It is also argued that fiscal consolidation can be expansionary (or increase economic growth) if it lowers expectations of future taxes, encouraging private spending.[28]

Many economists agree, however, that these programs are costly to implement. They argue that austerity policies reduce aggregate demand in the short term, causing the economy to contract and unemployment to increase.[29] This is why austerity programs are often also called contractionary policies. Additionally, they argue that if economic output falls at a faster rate than the debt does, the ratio of debt to GDP can actually rise, failing to address effectively the government's debt burden. Finally, austerity programs can be politically difficult to implement, as anti-austerity protests in a number of countries, including Belgium, Greece, Ireland, and Spain, among others, demonstrate.[30]

Some contend that financial assistance from other governments or the IMF can help ease the contractionary effects of fiscal consolidation, by allowing austerity reforms to occur over a longer time frame than they would otherwise have to occur. However, because the financial assistance provided by the IMF, as well as from the European countries in the case of Greece, Ireland, and Portugal, takes the form of loans, others argue that this financial assistance only exacerbates the country's problems and leads to ever-increasing debt levels.

Debt Restructuring

Debt restructuring refers to reorganizing a debt that has become too large and burdensome for the borrower to manage.[31] It can refer to providing more lenient terms about how a debt will be repaid, such as extending the time period over which the debt will be repaid (the maturity of the loan) or lowering the interest rate. It can also refer to a reduction in (or forgiveness of some of) the outstanding balance or principal. In either case, it means that the current owners of the debt get less than they were originally promised.[32] Debt restructurings are unusual but not unprecedented. Several emerging markets restructured their debt in the late 1990s and 2000s, including Russia and Argentina, among others.[33]

Proponents of debt restructuring argue that it is a way for governments to reduce their debt burden while limiting the austerity measures imposed on their citizens. Instead, it pushes the cost

---

[27] For example, see Alberto Alesina, *Fiscal Adjustments: Lessons from Recent History*, Working Paper, April 2010, http://www.economics.harvard.edu/faculty/alesina/files/Fiscal%2BAdjustments_lessons.pdf.

[28] For example, see Francesco Giavazzi and Marco Pagano, *Can Severe Fiscal Contractions be Expansionary? Tales of Two Small European Countries*, NBER Working Paper, No. 3372, May 1990, http://www.nber.org/papers/w3372.

[29] For example, see discussion of Keynesian economics in International Monetary Fund, *World Economic Outlook*, October 2010, Chapter 3: "Will It Hurt? Macroeconomic Effects of Fiscal Consolidation," http://www.imf.org/external/pubs/ft/weo/2010/02/pdf/c3.pdf.

[30] For example, see "European Cities Hit by Anti-Austerity Protests," *BBC News Europe*, September 25, 2010, http://www.bbc.co.uk/news/world-europe-11432579.

[31] Lex Rieffel, *Restructuring Sovereign Debt: The Case for Ad Hoc Machinery* (Washington, DC: Brookings Institution Press, 2003).

[32] Martin Feldstein, "Why Greece Will Default," *Business Insider*, April 10, 2010, http://www.businessinsider.com/why-greece-will-default-2010-4.

[33] Federico Sturzenegger and Jeromin Zettelmeyer, *Debt Defaults and Lessons from a Decade of Crises* (Cambridge, MA: MIT Press, 2007).

of debt reduction onto private creditors, who, some argue, should bear the consequences of taking on higher risk in exchange for greater potential reward.[34]

Critics argue that restructuring is not a desirable option for lowering debt burdens. Economists at the IMF, for example, have said that debt restructuring among advanced economies is "unnecessary, undesirable, and unlikely."[35] For some advanced economies, a large share of government debt is held domestically. This suggests that imposing losses on private creditors instead of implementing austerity measures may not shield the government from domestic backlash. Also, governments may have trouble borrowing from capital markets after restructuring their debt, meaning that they would need to bring their government budgets into balance or surplus more quickly than if they had not restructured.[36] Or they may face higher interest rates, making borrowing more costly.

The logistics of debt restructuring can also be difficult. Organizing and negotiating with potentially thousands of individual bondholders can be cumbersome and time-consuming, although recent changes in the legal processes related to sovereign bonds have helped streamline restructuring.[37] Finally, debt restructuring may be undesirable because it can increase investor anxiety and cause the crisis to spread to other countries. For example, with the Eurozone crisis, the European countries and the IMF are working to keep the crisis from spreading from the relatively small economies of Greece, Ireland, and Portugal to larger economies in the region, including Spain, Italy, or Belgium.

Inflation

If sovereign debt is denominated in the domestic currency, the government can use inflation to reduce the real value of the debt. This is frequently referred to as a government "running the printing presses" in order to create the money it needs to repay creditors, although there are other ways the government can create inflation in the economy. Many economists view this policy as an effective default on the debt, because even if creditors are repaid, the value of goods and services they can purchase is significantly lower than what they expected when they extended the loan to the government. Inflation has not featured prominently in recent major emerging-market debt crises because most emerging-market debt tends to be denominated in foreign currencies.[38]

---

[34] Arvind Subramanian, "Greek Deal Lets Banks Off the Hook," *Financial Times*, May 6, 2010.

[35] Carlo Cottarelli, Lorenzo Forni, and Jan Gottschalk, et al., *Default in Today's Advanced Economies: Unnecessary, Undesirable, and Unlikely*, IMF Staff Position Note, September 1, 2010, http://www.imf.org/external/pubs/ft/spn/2010/spn1012.pdf.

[36] However, some argue that governments that have defaulted can regain access to capital markets by successfully concluding a debt restructuring. See Federico Sturzenegger and Jeromin Zettelmeyer, *Debt Defaults and Lessons from a Decade of Crises* (Cambridge, MA: MIT Press, 2007), pp. 50.

[37] Specifically, the inclusion of "collective action clauses" (CACs) in sovereign bonds, which became popular in the 2000s, has helped expedite the restructuring process. CACs allow a supermajority of bondholders (usually 75%) to agree to a debt restructuring that is legally binding on all bondholders. Without CACs, some bondholders may have incentives to try to hold out for better terms, slowing down the negotiations. For more information on CACs, see, for example, Federal Reserve Bank of San Francisco, "Resolving Sovereign Debt Crises with Collective Action Clauses," Economic Letter No. 2004-06 (February 20, 2004), http://www.frbsf.org/publications/economics/letter/2004/el2004-06.pdf.

[38] Inflation has reduced the real value of domestic public debt in some emerging economies in recent decades, including Argentina, Brazil, and Turkey in the late 1980s and 1990s. Domestic public debt crises, however, tend to garner less international attention than external public debt crises. There is a long history of countries using inflation to address (continued...)

Inflation allows a government to repay its debt without having to implement austerity measures, and can be less complicated than a debt restructuring. Using inflation as part of a debt management strategy, however, can be problematic. The inflation has to be unexpected to investors, or else investors will price in the risk of inflation through higher interest rates. Even if the government is able to introduce surprise inflation, it will raise the government's borrowing costs in the future. Inflation can also have a number of adverse consequences, including wiping out the value of savings, creating shortages of goods, and reducing future investment by creating uncertainty in the economy. Governments may also have trouble limiting the amount of inflation introduced into the economy: one round of inflation may raise expectations about future inflation, which in turn could lead to more inflation. Additionally, using inflation to lower the real value of the debt assumes the cooperation of the central bank, but in most advanced economies, the central bank sets policies independently of the government. Finally, using inflation to address a debt problem is not available to countries whose debt is denominated in a currency held jointly. Individual Eurozone countries issue debt denominated in euros, but they do not have control over monetary policy in the Eurozone and cannot use inflation to reduce the real value of their debt.

Growth

Economic growth also allows governments to lower the size of their debt relative to the size of their economy (typically measured as gross domestic product [GDP]). It can also lead to lower levels of government spending and increase tax revenues, lowering the dollar value of sovereign debt as well. In the short run, economic stabilization is a necessary condition for sustained economic growth. Growth can be stimulated by pursuing expansionary fiscal and monetary policies or by pursuing structural reforms at the microeconomic level. Expansionary fiscal policies, however, lead to more debt, and "easy" monetary policies, such as lowering interest rates, may not be effective if firms and households are unwilling to borrow to increase investment and consumption. At the microeconomic level, growth can be supported by a number of structural reforms that can increase the competitiveness of industries in the economy. Examples include removing barriers to labor mobility, privatizing state-owned companies, and liberalizing trade policy. The IMF's program for Greece, for example, includes structural reforms aimed at encouraging growth.

The benefit of growing out of debt is that it allows countries to address their debt problems without possibly painful fiscal cuts or alienating creditors. However, the results of these reforms tend to manifest themselves over the long term, and a country already in a debt crisis may have difficulty just "growing out of it" in the short term. Moreover, empirical evidence suggests that countries with high levels of debt have trouble growing.[39] The uncertainty around growth as a strategy for short-term debt reduction is one reason why Greece's IMF program does not just include structural reforms; fiscal cuts are also a central component.

(...continued)

debt levels, with numerous examples from medieval Europe and as far back as Greece in fourth century B.C. See Carmen Reinhart and Kenneth Rogoff, *This Time Is Different: Eight Centuries of Financial Folly* (Princeton, NJ: Princeton University Press, 2009), chapter 8, "Domestic Debt: The Missing Link Explaining External Default and High Inflation," and chapter 11, "Default Through Debasement: An 'Old World' Favorite."

[39] Carmen Reinhart and Kenneth Rogoff, "Growth in a Time of Debt," *American Economic Review*, vol. 100, no. 2 (May 2010).

Financial Repression

Some economists argue that governments can also use financial repression to lower debt levels.[40] "Financial repression" generally refers to the use of government policies to induce or force domestic investors to buy government bonds at artificially low interest rates. Specifically, they sell bonds at interest rates below the rate of inflation, meaning that the real interest rate (the interest rate adjusted for inflation) is negative. All else being equal, extending loans with negative real interest rates results in falling debt-to-GDP ratios over time. In order to get investors to buy these bonds, governments use a host of policies, such as restrictions on the outflow of capital, to create a captive domestic audience for these bonds. For example, governments may require pension funds to hold government bonds.

Empirical evidence indicates that financial repression was used by several advanced economies to lower public debt levels following World War II.[41] It is estimated that real interest rates in advanced countries were negative roughly half the time between 1945 and 1980. Some economists estimate that, in the United States and United Kingdom, financial repression helped reduce debt levels by 3%-4% of GDP a year, or 30% to 40% each decade between the end of World War II and the 1970s.

Financial repression may be attractive because it avoids many of the pitfalls of the other policy options for lowering debt levels: it avoids politically painful austerity measures, is arguably less disruptive than debt restructuring, does not require introducing surprise inflation into the economy, and is a more certain policy option than growth. Thirty years of financial liberalization, however, have made it technically difficult for governments to return to the capital controls necessary to embark on a policy agenda of financial repression.[42] Policy-makers may also have trouble imposing the controls before capital flight takes place, and the controls could damage a country's ability to attract foreign investment. Financial repression may also be politically difficult, as investors would likely oppose policies that restrict their investment opportunities or require them to buy government bonds at artificially low interest rates.

Current Strategies

The primary policy response across advanced economies to historically high debt levels has been fiscal austerity. Several advanced economies have announced austerity measures, some, such as Greece, Ireland, and Portugal, in response to market pressures, and others, such as the United Kingdom, ahead of changes in investor sentiment. At the G-20 summit in June 2010 in Toronto, governments of advanced economies pledged to halve deficits by 2013 and stabilize or reduce government debt-to-GDP ratios by 2016.[43] However, G-20 commitments are not binding, and there has been little discussion of commitments for fiscal consolidation in subsequent G-20 summits.

---

[40] For example, see Carmen Reinhart and M. Belen Sbrancia, *The Liquidation of Government Debt*, NBER Working Paper, No. 16893, March 2011, http://www.imf.org/external/np/seminars/eng/2011/res2/pdf/crbs.pdf. Also see Gillian Tett, "Policymakers Learn a New and Alarming Catchphrase," *Financial Times*, May 9, 2011.

[41] Ibid.

[42] "Locking Up Your Money," *The Economist*, May 4, 2011.

[43] For more on the G-20, see CRS Report R40977, *The G-20 and International Economic Cooperation: Background and Implications for Congress*, by Rebecca M. Nelson. For the Toronto summit declaration, see http://www.g20.org/Documents/g20_declaration_en.pdf.

One notable exception is Japan, whose plans to consolidate finances was derailed in March 2011 by an earthquake, tsunami, and ensuing nuclear crisis. The physical damage is estimated to be between $195 billion and $305 billion, and the crisis created the need for immediate spending to cover reconstruction costs. As the government borrows to finance reconstruction, Japan's public debt, which is already one of the highest among advanced economies, is expected to rise.

In addition to austerity measures in most advanced economies, in March 2012, the Greek government implemented what is being called the largest debt restructuring in history. About 97% of privately held Greek bonds (about €197 billion, or about $256 billion) took a 53.5% cut to the face value (principal) of the bond, and the net present value of the bonds was reduced by approximately 75%. However, even with the restructuring, a sharp economic contraction in Greece has exacerbated public finances, and its debt to GDP ratio is forecasted by the IMF to be 171% of GDP in 2012, which many economists fear is still too high. Further debt relief, particularly from "official" creditors (other European governments), could be necessary.

Some economists are concerned that the emphasis on austerity measures could undermine a fragile global economic recovery, particularly while unemployment remains high in many advanced economies. Others argue that the announced fiscal consolidation plans do not go far enough, and are concerned that there will not be sufficient political will to undertake the reforms necessary to stabilize and reduce debt levels over the long term.

Issues for Congress

Is the United States Headed for a Eurozone-Style Debt Crisis?

Some analysts,[44] as well as some Members of Congress, have expressed concern that the United States is headed towards a debt crisis similar to those experienced by some Eurozone countries, including Greece, Ireland, and Portugal. They are concerned about loss of investor confidence and the loss of the United States' ability to borrow at reasonable interest rates. Like these Eurozone countries, it is argued, the United States has been reliant on foreign investors to fund a large budget deficit, resulting in rising debt levels and increasing vulnerability to a sudden reversal in investor confidence. S&P's downgrade of long-term U.S. debt in August 2011 reinforced concerns about the U.S. commitment and ability to repay its debt.

Other economists argue that the U.S. debt position is much stronger than that of the Eurozone economies in crisis.[45] Unlike Greece, Portugal, and Ireland, the United States has a floating exchange rate and its currency is an international reserve currency, which can alleviate many of the pressures associated with rising debt levels.[46] Additionally, they argue that the stronger levels of economic growth and the lower borrowing costs of the United States put U.S. debt levels on a more sustainable path over time. Even with the S&P downgrade, the U.S. credit rating is still higher than the crisis countries. The United States also has a strong historical record of debt

---

[44] For example, see Niall Ferguson, "A Greek Crisis is Coming to America," *Financial Times*, February 10, 2010.

[45] For example, see Paul Krugman, "We're Not Greece," *New York Times*, May 10, 2010.

[46] For example, a depreciation in the dollar relative to other countries can bolster exports and spur growth, offsetting the effects of austerity. Likewise, the dollar's status as an international reserve makes it a safe haven for investments during times of distress or crisis, bolstering demand for government bonds even as debt levels are rising.

repayment that helps bolster its reputation in capital markets. Greece, by contrast, has been in a state of default about 50% of the time since independence in the 1830s.[47]

Bond market data indicate that investors do not view the United States in a similar light to Greece, Ireland, or Portugal. **Figure 5** compares the spreads on Greek, Irish, Portuguese, U.S., and UK 10-year bonds (over 10-year German bonds) since 2008. Higher bond spreads indicate higher levels of risk. U.S. bond spreads have remained substantially lower than Greek, Irish, and Portuguese bond spreads throughout the Eurozone crisis. U.S. bond spreads have been much closer in value to UK bond spreads, even during the financial crisis that originated in the U.S. housing market.

Figure 5. Bond Spreads for Selected Advanced Economies

Spreads on 10-year bonds over German 10-year bonds

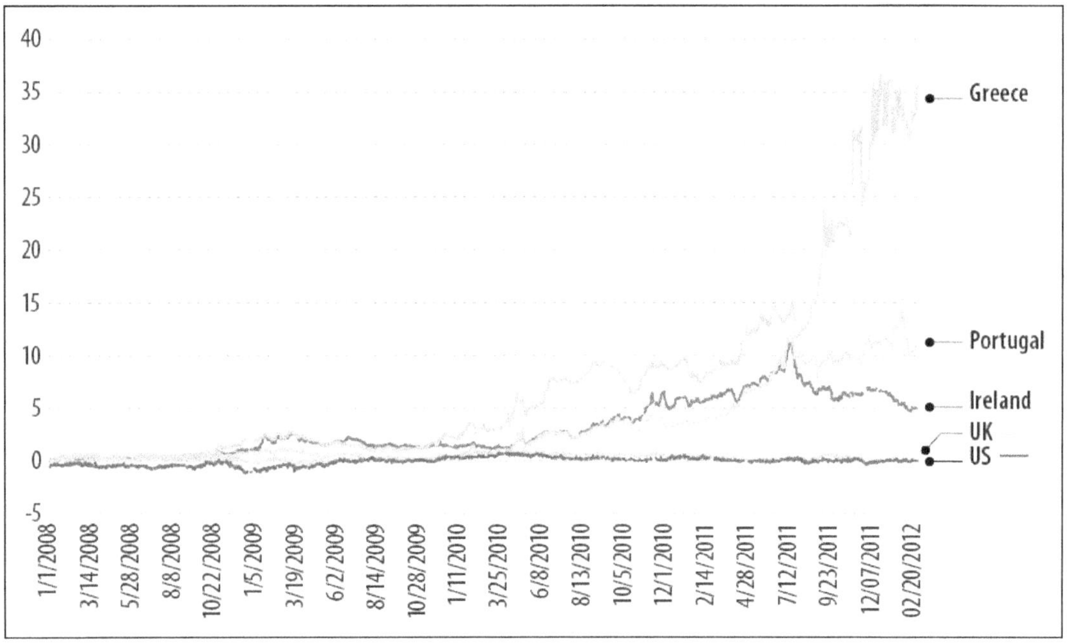

Source: Global Financial Data.

Additionally, one market research firm (Credit Market Analysis, CMA) estimates the likelihood of default over the next five years for a number of governments, and publishes the top 10 most and least risky sovereigns on a quarterly basis. For the fourth quarter of 2012, it estimated the likelihood of the United States defaulting on its debt over the next five years to be 3.30%, and ranks the United States as the fifth least-likely country to default. By contrast, Cyprus, Portugal, and Spain are all ranked in the top 10 countries most likely to default. (Data was not availalbe for calculating Greece's probability of default; see note in **Table 1**.) CMA estimates that Cyprus is more likely to default than not over the next 5 years, with an estimated probability of default of 60.5%.

---

[47] See Carmen Reinhart and Kenneth Rogoff, *This Time Is Different: Eight Centuries of Financial Folly* (Princeton, NJ: Princeton University Press, 2009), Table 6.6.

Table 1. Market Estimates of the Likelihood of Sovereign Defaults
2012 Q4

Highest Probability of Default			Lowest Probability of Default		
1.	Argentina	61.4%	1.	Sweden	1.64
2.	Cyprus	60.5	2.	Norway	1.72
3.	Pakistan	42.8	3.	Finland	2.64
4.	Venezuela	37.4	4.	Denmark	2.94
5.	Ukraine	36.3	**5.**	**United States**	**3.30**
6.	Portugal	32.3	6.	UK	3.66
7.	Egypt	30.4	6.	Germany	3.66
8.	Iraq	28.1	8.	Switzerland	3.77
9.	Lebanon	27.5	9.	Austria	3.96
10.	Spain	23.5	10.	Netherlands	4.04

Source: Credit Market Analysis (CMA), "CMA Global Sovereign Debt Credit Risk Report," Q4 2012, http://www.cmavision.com/images/uploads/docs/CMA_Global_Sovereign_Debt_Credit_Risk_Report_Q4_2012.pdf.

Note: Likelihood of default over the next five years. Calculations based on credit default swap (CDS) values, and due to thin trading on Greek CDS, its probability of default was not available this quarter.

Markets may perceive the United States favorably not because they believe the deficits are currently at sustainable levels but because they believe that the government will implement policies that reduce the deficit. However, it is important to note that market perceptions can change quickly, and it can be difficult to predict when markets can lose confidence.

Implications for the U.S. Economy

How other advanced economies address their debt levels has implications for the U.S. economy. Most advanced economies are addressing high debt levels through fiscal austerity. If large austerity packages in advanced economies slow growth in those countries, demand for U.S. exports could fall. Because advanced economies are major trading partners of the United States, this could impact U.S. exports. Slower growth rates in advanced economies could make investment there less attractive, and could lead to U.S. investors shifting their investment portfolios away from advanced economies and toward emerging markets. Investors in those countries also could shift their portfolios away from U.S. debt.

If any advanced economies do default, restructure their public debt, or use inflation to reduce the real value of their debt, U.S. investors could face losses on their investments. **Figure 6** shows where U.S. banks have credit committed directly to borrowers overseas in general, not just to sovereign borrowers—also referred to as how heavily U.S. banks are "exposed" overseas. Direct U.S. bank exposure in general is more heavily concentrated among advanced economies than emerging and developing countries. As of September 2012, 72% ($2,353 billion of $3,277 billion) of U.S. bank exposure overseas was concentrated in advanced economies.[48] Among

---

[48] Data on bank exposure from Bank for International Settlements (BIS) for September 2010. See **Figure 6** source and notes for more details.

advanced economies, U.S. banks were most exposed to the United Kingdom ($633 billion), Japan ($380 billion), Germany ($221 billion), France ($216 billion), and Canada ($128 billion) in September 2012.

Figure 6. Direct Exposure of U.S. Banks to Advanced Economies

September 2012

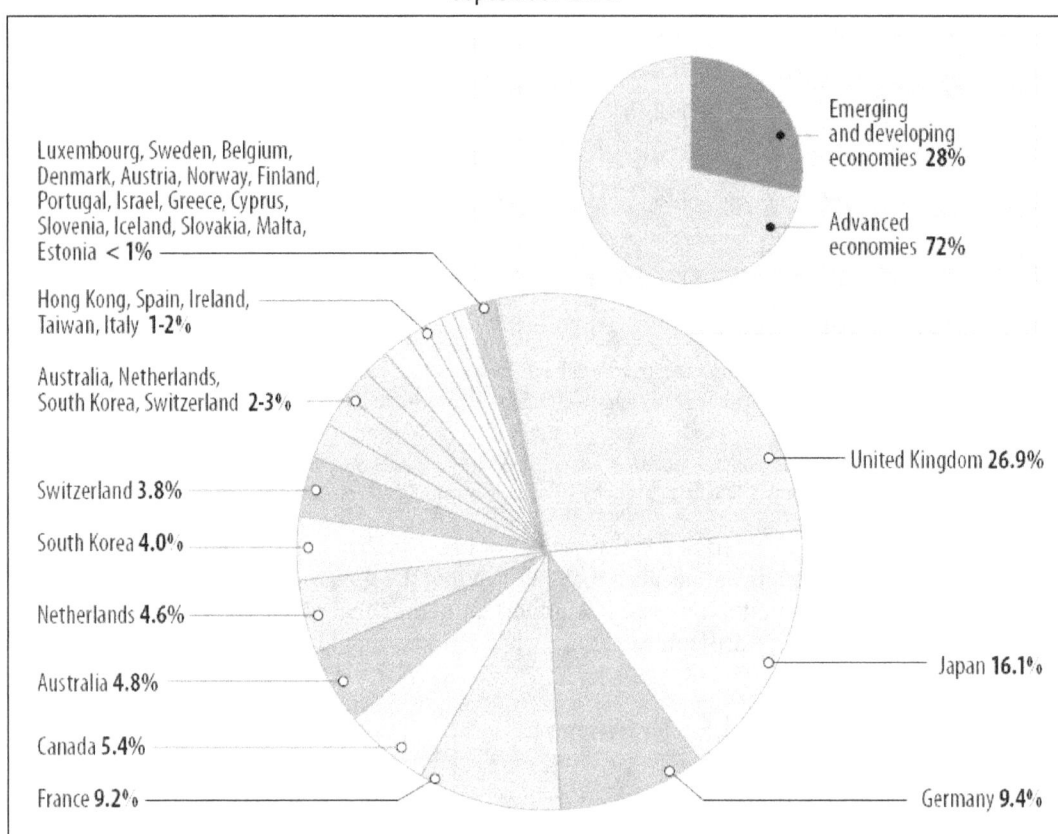

Source: Bank for International Settlements (BIS), "Consolidated International Claims of BIS Reporting Banks," January 2013, preliminary data, Table 9D, "Consolidated Foreign Claims of Reporting Banks—Ultimate Risk Basis," http://www.bis.org./statistics/consstats.htm.

Note: Direct bank lending only, and exposure to the economy overall (government and private sector). Data do not include exposure of U.S. financial institutions through the issuance of credit default swaps based on sovereign debt, which could lower or raise U.S. bank exposure. They also do not consider secondary exposures (i.e., for U.S. banks exposed to the United Kingdom, who, in turn, the United Kingdom is exposed to, such as Ireland). Countries listed as advanced economies are identified as such by the IMF in the *World Economic Outlook*, September 2011. See **Table A-3** for exposure in dollar terms.

Direct exposure of U.S. banks to the Eurozone countries that have come under the most intense market pressure to date—Greece, Ireland, and Portugal—is relatively small. According to the Bank for International Settlements (BIS), U.S. bank exposure to these three countries, including the sovereign and private sector, totaled $54 billion in September 2012, or 1.6% of direct U.S. bank exposure overseas. Direct U.S. bank exposure to Italy and Spain (sovereign and private sector) totaled an additional $89 billion. Some of these losses could already have been absorbed in bank balance sheets if they are marking investments to market.

In addition to data on direct U.S. bank exposures, the BIS has recently started publishing data on banks' "other potential exposures" overseas, which include derivative contracts, guarantees extended, and credit commitments. U.S. "other potential exposures" to Greece, Ireland, Italy, Portugal, and Spain (sovereign and private sector) totaled $625 billion in September 2012. However, the BIS data does not capture any collateral or hedges that U.S. banks may have in place to lower their exposure to a particular borrower, and some argue that this BIS data overstates the risks of U.S. banks. Others argue that it is helpful measure, because the amount and quality of collateral is not publicly known, and that it captures the risk facing U.S. banks in a systemic financial crisis where U.S. banks' counterparties on hedging agreements could fail.

BIS data capture the exposure of banking institutions, and do not include the exposures of other financial institutions, such as money market, insurance, and pension funds. They also do not capture secondary exposures, such as U.S. banks that are exposed to UK banks, which are in turn exposed to Ireland. Overall, there is a high level of uncertainty surrounding the full exposure of the U.S. financial system to Eurozone countries under market pressure, and uncertainty surrounding the full implications of a default or restructuring, particularly if it triggers contagion, for the U.S. financial system.

Policy Options for Congress

Most advanced economies, including the United States, have focused on addressing high debt levels through fiscal austerity. The task facing these countries is how to pursue fiscal consolidation without derailing economic recovery. How to do this is contentious and has sparked debates within Congress and more generally at the multilateral level.

Some argue that the most helpful course of action in the U.S. Congress is to fix its own fiscal problems, although there is disagreement on the appropriate pace of and measures for achieving fiscal consolidation. Additionally, some argue that Congress can urge the Administration to address the issues related to historically high levels of sovereign debt issues in multilateral discussions, particularly in the context of the G-20 and the international financial institutions (IFIs).[49] Generally, there may be multilateral interest in coordinating fiscal policies in order to prevent large simultaneous fiscal contractions among all the advanced economies, which could lower demand in the advanced economies and undermine a fragile economic recovery. Coordinating fiscal policies, such as encouraging advanced countries that do not have debt problems to pursue more expansionary fiscal policies, could soften the impact of austerity in countries with unsustainable debt levels on the global economy. The G-20 and its process of assessing the compatibility of policies across countries (the "mutual assessment process" [MAP]) could be one forum for these discussions.[50] There may also be interest in revisiting the G-20 commitments for fiscal consolidation pledged by the advanced economies at the Toronto summit in June 2010, and momentum may be building in the G-20 to discuss the Eurozone debt crisis.

Congress may also urge the Administration to engage with the IFIs, such as the IMF, on the challenges posed by high debt levels in advanced economies. The IMF already analyzes fiscal policies and debt levels in its semiannual fiscal monitor reports. However, IFI engagement on this

---

[49] For more on the G-20 and the mutual assessment process, see CRS Report R40977, *The G-20 and International Economic Cooperation: Background and Implications for Congress*, by Rebecca M. Nelson.

[50] The G-20 Toronto declaration is available at http://www.g20.org/Documents/g20_declaration_en.pdf.

issue could increase. Following sovereign debt crises in the emerging markets, the IMF and the World Bank launched an initiative to systematically collect public debt data on a quarterly basis.[51] The purpose of the initiative is to increase transparency about public-sector debt by facilitating timely dissemination of standardized public debt data. Thirty-eight emerging markets provide data to the project. Extending participation to advanced economies could help further increase transparency about public debt levels in these major economies as well.

---

[51] Specifically, they launched the Public Sector Debt Statistics (PSD) database. See http://go.worldbank.org/9PIAZORON0.

Appendix. Data on General Government Debt and U.S. Bank Exposure Overseas

Table A-1. Gross General Government Debt in Advanced Economies, Actual and Forecasts

% of GDP

Country	1980	1990	2000	2006	2007	2008	2009	2010	2011	2012	2013	2014	2015	2016
Australia	n/a	16.4	19.5	10.0	9.7	11.8	16.9	20.5	24.2	27.1	27.2	26.4	24.7	22.9
Austria	n/a	56.2	66.2	62.3	60.2	63.8	69.2	71.8	72.3	74.3	74.9	74.4	73.0	71.6
Belgium	74.3	125.6	107.8	88.0	84.0	89.3	95.7	95.6	97.8	99.0	99.4	98.6	96.5	93.9
Canada	45.6	75.2	82.1	70.3	66.5	71.3	83.3	85.1	85.4	87.5	87.8	84.6	82.3	80.3
Cyprus	n/a	n/a	59.6	64.7	58.8	48.9	58.5	61.5	71.6	87.3	92.6	97.6	101.6	104.1
Czech Republic	n/a	n/a	17.8	28.3	28.0	28.7	34.3	37.6	40.5	43.1	45.0	45.6	45.7	45.7
Denmark	n/a	n/a	60.4	41.0	34.1	41.9	40.6	42.9	44.1	47.1	47.6	47.8	47.9	47.3
Estonia	n/a	n/a	5.1	4.4	3.7	4.5	7.2	6.7	6.0	8.2	9.7	9.3	8.7	8.2
Finland	10.8	13.8	43.8	39.6	35.2	33.9	43.5	48.6	49.1	52.6	53.9	54.1	53.6	52.7
France	20.7	35.2	57.4	64.1	64.2	68.2	79.2	82.3	86.0	90.0	92.1	92.9	92.3	90.1
Germany	n/a	n/a	60.2	67.9	65.4	66.9	74.7	82.4	80.6	83.0	81.5	79.6	77.6	75.8
Greece	22.6	73.3	103.4	107.3	107.4	112.6	129.0	144.6	165.4	170.7	181.8	180.2	174.0	164.1
Hong Kong	n/a	n/a	n/a	33.0	32.8	30.6	33.2	34.6	33.8	33.1	31.0	30.4	29.7	29.1
Iceland	25.5	36.2	41.0	30.1	29.1	70.3	88.2	92.8	99.2	94.2	90.5	87.4	84.0	78.6
Ireland	65.2	93.5	37.5	24.8	25.0	44.5	64.9	92.2	106.5	117.7	119.3	118.4	115.0	111.5
Israel	n/a	n/a	84.3	84.7	78.1	77.0	79.4	76.0	74.1	73.3	72.9	71.8	70.5	68.9
Italy	n/a	94.3	108.5	106.1	103.1	105.7	116.0	118.6	120.1	126.3	127.8	127.3	125.6	123.3
Japan	50.6	67.0	140.1	186.0	183.0	191.8	210.2	215.3	229.6	236.6	245.0	246.2	247.6	248.8
Korea	n/a	13.8	18.0	31.1	30.7	30.1	33.8	33.4	34.2	33.5	31.6	29.4	27.2	25.2
Luxembourg	n/a	n/a	6.2	6.7	6.7	13.7	14.8	19.1	18.2	21.7	24.6	27.3	30.9	33.9
Malta	n/a	n/a	57.9	64.2	62.2	62.2	67.8	69.1	71.6	71.8	71.1	69.7	67.8	65.5

Country	1980	1990	2000	2006	2007	2008	2009	2010	2011	2012	2013	2014	2015	2016
Netherlands	n/a	n/a	53.8	47.4	45.3	58.5	60.8	62.9	65.2	68.2	70.2	71.9	72.7	73.8
New Zealand	n/a	58.9	31.8	19.4	17.3	20.2	26.2	32.5	38.2	38.6	38.1	37.9	36.1	35.7
Norway	47.3	28.9	32.7	59.0	56.8	54.3	48.9	49.6	49.6	49.6	49.6	49.6	49.6	49.6
Portugal	n/a	57.2	48.4	63.7	68.3	71.6	83.1	93.3	107.8	119.1	123.7	123.6	120.8	117.6
Singapore	n/a	71.1	81.2	86.4	85.8	96.9	103.4	101.2	107.6	106.2	103.4	100.8	97.8	95.1
Slovak Republic	n/a	n/a	50.3	30.5	29.6	27.9	35.6	41.1	43.3	46.3	47.2	47.6	48.1	48.4
Slovenia	n/a	n/a	29.5	26.4	23.1	22.0	35.0	38.6	46.9	53.2	57.4	58.7	59.2	59.1
Spain	16.6	42.5	59.4	39.7	36.3	40.2	53.9	61.3	69.1	90.7	96.9	100.0	101.1	101.4
Sweden	n/a	n/a	53.3	44.8	39.7	38.4	42.0	38.8	37.9	37.1	35.9	34.1	31.0	27.7
Switzerland	n/a	37.3	59.9	62.4	55.6	50.5	51.8	48.0	46.8	46.7	45.6	43.6	42.6	42.3
Taiwan	n/a	n/a	26.6	34.2	33.3	34.7	38.0	38.1	40.5	41.7	40.9	39.8	37.5	35.2
United Kingdom	46.1	32.4	40.9	43.0	43.7	52.2	68.0	75.0	81.8	88.7	93.3	96.0	96.6	95.8
United States	42.3	63.9	54.8	66.6	67.2	76.1	89.7	98.6	102.9	107.2	111.7	113.8	114.2	114.2
Advanced economies	n/a	n/a	72.5	76.6	74.0	81.0	94.5	100.6	104.7	109.9	112.7	113.2	112.7	111.8
G-7 advanced economies	n/a	n/a	77.3	85.5	83.5	91.8	107.0	114.7	119.9	125.1	128.8	129.7	129.4	128.7
Emerging and developing economies	n/a	n/a	48.6	36.5	34.7	32.6	35.7	39.5	36.3	34.4	32.7	31.5	30.5	29.4

Source: *IMF World Economic Outlook*, October 2012.

Note: Forecasted data starts in 2009 or later, depending on the country. n/a = not available.

Table A-2. Net General Government Debt in Advanced Economies, Actual and Forecasts

% of GDP

Country	1980	1990	2000	2006	2007	2008	2009	2010	2011	2012	2013	2014	2015	2016
Australia	n/a	9.6	7.1	-6.3	-7.3	-5.3	-0.6	4.0	8.2	11.6	12.4	12.3	11.3	10.2
Austria	n/a	36.7	43.2	43.1	40.9	42.0	49.2	52.5	52.1	54.1	54.7	54.1	52.8	51.4
Belgium	65.5	112.3	97.4	77.0	73.1	73.4	79.6	79.8	81.4	82.9	83.6	83.1	81.5	79.3
Canada	14.5	43.7	46.2	26.3	22.9	22.4	28.3	30.4	33.1	35.8	37.5	38.1	37.8	37.1
Cyprus	n/a	n/a	n/a	n/a	n/a	n/a	n/a	n/a	n/a	n/a	n/a	n/a	n/a	n/a
Czech Republic	n/a	n/a	n/a	n/a	n/a	n/a	n/a	n/a	n/a	n/a	n/a	n/a	n/a	n/a
Denmark	n/a	n/a	22.5	1.9	-3.8	-6.1	-4.5	-1.7	0.2	4.1	6.0	7.6	9.2	10.0
Estonia	n/a	n/a	3.3	-4.9	-5.7	-3.5	-1.2	-1.8	-0.2	4.3	5.1	5.3	4.8	3.9
Finland	-177.1	-208.3	-31.1	-69.4	-72.5	-52.3	-62.8	-65.5	-54.1	-51.1	-48.1	-45.7	-43.8	-42.4
France	n/a	25.4	51.4	59.6	59.6	62.3	72.0	76.1	78.8	83.7	85.9	86.7	86.1	83.9
Germany	n/a	n/a	41.1	53.0	50.5	50.2	57.0	56.2	55.3	58.4	57.5	56.2	56.2	56.2
Greece	20.6	64.2	77.4	107.3	107.4	112.6	129.0	144.6	165.4	170.7	181.8	180.2	174.0	164.1
Hong Kong	n/a	n/a	n/a	n/a	n/a	n/a	n/a	n/a	n/a	n/a	n/a	n/a	n/a	n/a
Iceland	3.3	19.0	24.3	7.8	10.8	41.8	55.8	62.8	65.9	65.7	64.4	62.4	59.3	55.8
Ireland	65.2	93.5	36.4	12.1	11.1	24.6	42.0	74.7	94.9	103.0	107.6	108.7	107.2	104.0
Israel	n/a	n/a	70.7	74.0	67.3	63.6	68.6	68.3	67.5	67.0	67.0	66.3	65.4	64.0
Italy	n/a	89.2	93.1	89.3	86.9	88.8	97.2	99.1	99.6	103.1	103.9	103.7	102.4	100.8
Japan	16.8	13.2	59.6	81.0	80.5	95.3	106.2	112.8	126.4	135.4	144.7	148.7	152.4	155.6
Korea	n/a	n/a	n/a	29.4	28.7	28.8	32.3	32.1	32.9	32.0	30.3	28.1	26.1	24.2
Luxembourg	n/a	n/a	n/a	n/a	n/a	n/a	n/a	n/a	n/a	n/a	n/a	n/a	n/a	n/a
Malta	n/a	n/a	n/a	n/a	n/a	n/a	n/a	n/a	n/a	n/a	n/a	n/a	n/a	n/a
Netherlands	n/a	n/a	24.9	24.5	21.6	20.6	23.2	27.6	31.7	35.1	37.6	40.2	42.1	44.1
New Zealand	n/a	46.5	18.2	0.2	-5.7	-4.8	-0.8	3.5	8.3	12.1	13.9	14.5	14.3	14.2
Norway	0.4	-31.8	-67.2	-133.7	-138.9	-123.5	-156.7	-165.3	-168.2	-169.3	-173.0	-178.3	-182.1	-184.5
Portugal	n/a	n/a	41.9	58.6	63.7	67.4	79.0	88.9	97.3	113.2	119.5	119.4	116.7	113.7

Country	1980	1990	2000	2006	2007	2008	2009	2010	2011	2012	2013	2014	2015	2016
Singapore	n/a	n/a	n/a	n/a	n/a	n/a	n/a	n/a	n/a	n/a	n/a	n/a	n/a	n/a
Slovak Republic	n/a	n/a	n/a	n/a	n/a	n/a	n/a	n/a	n/a	n/a	n/a	n/a	n/a	n/a
Slovenia	n/a	n/a	n/a	n/a	n/a	n/a	n/a	n/a	n/a	n/a	n/a	n/a	n/a	n/a
Spain	n/a	30.3	50.4	30.7	26.7	30.8	42.5	49.8	57.5	78.6	84.4	87.3	88.3	88.5
Sweden	n/a	n/a	2.2	-13.8	-17.3	-12.4	-19.4	-20.6	-18.2	-17.5	-16.5	-16.0	-16.9	-18.2
Switzerland	n/a	14.2	37.0	39.7	32.0	28.0	28.7	25.7	25.9	25.8	25.2	24.1	23.6	23.4
Taiwan	n/a	n/a	n/a	n/a	n/a	n/a	n/a	n/a	n/a	n/a	n/a	n/a	n/a	n/a
United Kingdom	40.5	26.5	33.6	37.8	38.0	45.8	60.6	71.0	76.6	83.7	88.2	90.9	91.5	90.7
United States	25.8	45.9	35.6	48.6	48.2	53.8	65.8	73.2	80.3	83.8	87.7	89.3	89.5	89.6
Advanced economies	n/a	n/a	43.6	48.3	46.3	51.6	62.0	66.6	71.6	76.5	79.7	80.9	81.2	81.2
G-7 advanced economies	n/a	n/a	45.7	55.6	54.6	60.8	72.2	77.9	84.1	89.0	92.8	94.3	94.9	95.0
Emerging and developing economies	n/a	n/a	n/a	n/a	n/a	n/a	n/a	n/a	n/a	n/a	n/a	n/a	n/a	n/a

Source: *IMF World Economic Outlook*, October 2012.

Note: Forecasted data starts in 2009 or later, depending on the country. n/a = not available.

Table A-3. Direct Exposure of U.S. Banks to Advanced Economies

September 2012, million US$

Country	Amount	Country	Amount	Country	Amount
Australia	113,654	Israel	4,027	Switzerland	89,688
Austria	12,410	Italy	39,726	Taiwan	40,059
Belgium	20,069	Japan	379,550	United Kingdom	632,994
Canada	127,674	Luxembourg	30,083		
Cyprus	1,502	Malta	181		
Czech Republic	19,393	Netherlands	108,443		
Denmark	40	New Zealand	10,750		
Estonia	10,140	Norway	5,102		
Finland	215,567	Portugal	594		
France	221,217	Singapore	1,000		
Germany	3,170	Slovakia	93,119		
Greece	52,091	Slovenia	49,268		
Hong Kong	699	South Korea	25,887		
Iceland	45,368	Spain	4,027		
Ireland	113,654	Sweden	39,726		
Advanced economies	2,353,465				
All countries	3,277,159				

Source: Bank for International Settlements (BIS), "Consolidated International Claims of BIS Reporting Banks," January 2013, preliminary data, Table 9D, "Consolidated Foreign Claims of Reporting Banks—Ultimate Risk Basis," http://www.bis.org./statistics/consstats.htm.

Note: Direct bank lending only, and exposure to the economy overall (government and private sector). Data do not include exposure of U.S. financial institutions through the issuance of credit default swaps based on sovereign debt, which could lower or raise U.S. bank exposure. They also do not consider secondary exposures (i.e., for U.S. banks exposed to the United Kingdom, who, in turn, the United Kingdom is exposed to, such as Ireland). Countries listed as advanced economies are identified as such by the IMF in the *World Economic Outlook* (excluding San Marino) .

Author Contact Information

Rebecca M. Nelson
Analyst in International Trade and Finance
rnelson@crs.loc.gov, 7-6819

Acknowledgments

Amber Wilhelm, Graphics Specialist, assisted in preparation of the figures.